SHARKS!

PHONICS

Sand Tiger Sharks

Book 10: nd-blends

By Quinlan B. Lee

Photo Credits: cover: Greg Amptman/Shutterstock; title page: Bill Curtsinger/National Geographic; pages 2-3: George Grall/National Geographic; page 4: Bill Curtsinger/National Geographic; pages 6-7: George Grall/National Geographic; pages 8-9: C. Fredrickson Photography/Getty Images; pages 10-11: Gerald Nowak/Media Bakery; pages 12-13: Greg Amptman/Shutterstock; pages 14-15: Juniors Bildarchiv/GmbH/Alamy; pages 16: Brian J. Skerry/National Geographic/Getty Images.

ISBN 978-0-545-74709-7

12 11 10 9 8 7 6 5 4 3 2 1   14 15 16 17 18/0

Printed in China   145

First Printing, September 2014

SCHOLASTIC INC.

Watch out for these sharks!
They look very scary.
Let's **find** out why they are
called **sand** tiger sharks.

These sharks like to be near the **land**.

They **tend** to **spend** time near the **sand** and waves.

That is why you **find** "**sand**" in their name.

Sand tiger sharks have gray and brown backs.
This is so they can **blend** in with the **sand**.

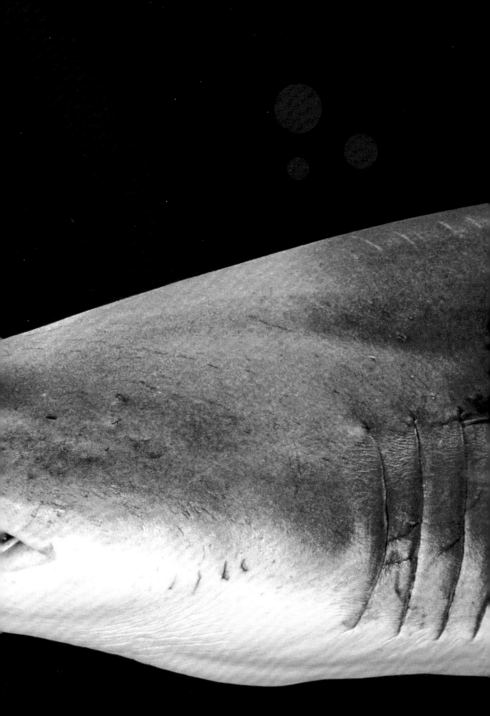

Why do you **find** "tiger" in their name?

Look at those teeth!

They are sharp on the **end**.

Do they look like tiger teeth to you?

Sand tiger sharks are the only **kind** of sharks that gulp air. They can float and **blend** in with the waves.

The fish don't see them until it is too late.

Chomp!

Would you like to **spend** time with a **sand** tiger shark? If you did, guess what you would **find** out?

Sand tiger sharks are usually slow and not the **kind** of sharks that bother people.

But if you are a fish,
watch out!

A **sand** tiger shark could **find**
you and that . . .

. . . would be the **end**!